# THIS IS ME! 2022

## POETRY FROM THE STARS

Edited By Reuben Messer

First published in Great Britain in 2022 by:

Young Writers
Remus House
Coltsfoot Drive
Peterborough
PE2 9BF
Telephone: 01733 890066
Website: www.youngwriters.co.uk

All Rights Reserved
Book Design by Ashley Janson
© Copyright Contributors 2022
Softback ISBN 978-1-80015-988-4

Printed and bound in the UK by BookPrintingUK
Website: www.bookprintinguk.com
YB0505L

# FOREWORD

For Young Writers' latest competition This Is Me, we asked primary school pupils to look inside themselves, to think about what makes them unique, and then write a poem about it! They rose to the challenge magnificently and the result is this fantastic collection of poems in a variety of poetic styles.

Here at Young Writers our aim is to encourage creativity in children and to inspire a love of the written word, so it's great to get such an amazing response, with some absolutely fantastic poems. It's important for children to focus on and celebrate themselves and this competition allowed them to write freely and honestly, celebrating what makes them great, expressing their hopes and fears, or simply writing about their favourite things. This Is Me gave them the power of words. The result is a collection of inspirational and moving poems that also showcase their creativity and writing ability.

I'd like to congratulate all the young poets in this anthology, I hope this inspires them to continue with their creative writing.

# CONTENTS

### Adamsrill Primary School, Sydenham

| | |
|---|---|
| Dalila Cortadellas Pascual (7) | 1 |
| Blythe Bell Lawrance (10) | 2 |
| Isla Pym (8) | 6 |
| Olive Yamaguchi-Crawley (10) | 8 |
| Lola Haywood Williams (9) | 10 |
| Stella Jean Collings (9) | 12 |
| Asher Bear (10) | 13 |
| Daniel (7) | 14 |
| Kayla Oluwatobi (9) | 15 |
| Shahid Abbas (8) | 16 |
| Eli | 17 |
| Amanda Abiana Nelson (10) | 18 |

### Bankton Primary School, Dedridge

| | |
|---|---|
| Ben Davidson (11) | 19 |
| Ethan Buendia (11) | 20 |
| Ava Mcadam (11) | 22 |
| Kacey Koo (11) | 23 |
| Kyle Robertson (11) | 24 |
| Robbie Vannet (11) | 25 |
| Miral Yousif (11) | 26 |
| Rayan Krouma (11) | 27 |
| Caleb Craig (11) | 28 |
| Leah Jack (11) | 29 |
| Fraser Haw (11) | 30 |
| Nathan Campbell (11) | 31 |
| Lauren Robertson (11) | 32 |
| Taiba Ali (10) | 33 |
| Mirren Brown (11) | 34 |
| Daniel Friis Jørgensen (11) | 35 |
| Cole Morrow (11) | 36 |

| | |
|---|---|
| Isla Mowatt (11) | 37 |
| Kayleigh Burrows | 38 |
| Daniel David Gough (12) | 39 |
| Nathan Snape (11) | 40 |

### Hasland Junior School, Hasland

| | |
|---|---|
| Erin Westwood (9) | 41 |
| Kacey Pell (10) | 42 |
| Ava Wilkinson (9) | 43 |
| Ellie May Lilly Pell (10) | 44 |
| Darwyn Steele (8) | 45 |

### Kirkshaws Primary School, Coatbridge

| | |
|---|---|
| Levent Kizilkaya (9) | 46 |
| Kayleigh Angela Cunningham (9) | 47 |
| Emily Paton (10) | 48 |
| Katie Paton (10) | 49 |
| Ethan Neville Madzinga (11) | 50 |
| Lucy Bannister (10) | 51 |
| Kiara Puiu (9) | 52 |

### Middleton Primary School, Leeds

| | |
|---|---|
| Zoe Williams (9) | 53 |
| Nathan Johnstone (10) | 54 |
| Mason Fletcher (10) | 55 |
| Dean Speake (11) | 56 |
| Mia Kalaszynska (9) | 57 |
| Emmanuella Mouanjo (9) | 58 |

## Rolleston Primary School, Glen Parva

| | |
|---|---|
| Eva Gilbert (9) | 59 |
| Frayer Sluggett (10) | 60 |
| Rosie Bond (9) | 61 |
| Isaac Wye (8) | 62 |
| Paria Mohamdi (10) | 63 |
| Daniel Derrett-Baugh (7) | 64 |
| Emilia Hinz (9) | 65 |
| Leo Carolan (8) | 66 |
| Alice Spence (8) | 67 |
| Isabella Maeve Robson (10) | 68 |
| Harley Mumford (8) | 69 |
| Ellie-Mae Pryor (9) | 70 |
| Charlie Lee Toon (9) | 71 |
| Darci Rae Rayns (8) | 72 |
| Lacey Mumford (10) | 73 |
| Jake Thomas (9) | 74 |
| Ayan Ben Grid (8) | 75 |
| Lexi Onions (8) | 76 |
| Abbey Corser Carlton (10) | 77 |
| Brea-Mae Battle (8) | 78 |
| Freddy | 79 |
| Charlie Frearson (7) | 80 |
| Preston Underwood (9) | 81 |
| Amelia Hancock (8) | 82 |
| Muaaz Imran (9) | 83 |
| Koby Keogh (9) | 84 |
| Bogdan Cernei (9) | 85 |
| Kyla Halifax (9) | 86 |
| Koben Smith (9) | 87 |
| Taryn Perkins (10) | 88 |
| Marley Wye (9) | 89 |
| Miley Moran (9) | 90 |
| Sarah Fatah (8) | 91 |
| Elisha Baines (8) | 92 |
| Oliver Redman (9) | 93 |
| Haira Ihsan (8) | 94 |
| Esmé Branstone (8) | 95 |
| Molly Smith (8) | 96 |
| Zayan Seedat (8) | 97 |
| Jesse Phillips (7) | 98 |

## Thorpe Lea Primary School, Thorpe Lea

| | |
|---|---|
| Tonny Barreto (11) | 99 |
| Pola Stankiewicz (9) | 100 |
| Ella Wells (10) | 101 |
| Madison Jones (8) | 102 |
| Rashida Moortasa (11) | 103 |
| Teagan West (9) | 104 |
| Rayyan Shah (9) | 105 |
| Layla Rose Stevens (11) | 106 |
| Allyna (9) | 107 |
| Maisie (9) | 108 |
| Lilly Rickwood (9) | 109 |
| Antonio Rebenciuc (10) | 110 |
| Abdul Rahman Ali (10) | 111 |
| Roman Bartram (9) | 112 |
| Freddy Breach (11) | 113 |
| Lola Williamson (10) | 114 |
| Finley William (8) | 115 |
| Poppy R (9) | 116 |
| Taylan Basaran (8) | 117 |
| Filip Bartosiak (8) | 118 |
| Alexis-May Hiley (8) | 119 |

## Unity Academy, Blackpool

| | |
|---|---|
| Lily Jayde Leeming (11) | 120 |
| Dylan Pace (11) | 121 |
| Bella Precious (10) | 122 |
| Lucia Panayiotis (11) | 123 |
| Harlee Saunders (11) | 124 |
| Tyler Cook (10) | 125 |
| Dylan Russell (11) | 126 |
| Freya Chennells (11) | 127 |
| Paddy Jones (11) | 128 |
| Elizer Oneall (11) | 129 |
| Dylan Fallows (11) | 130 |
| Keeley Royle (11) | 131 |
| Tillie Gilbert (10) | 132 |
| Domonic Woodall (10) | 133 |
| Marika Pokule (10) | 134 |
| Madeleine Green (10) | 135 |
| Emily Moore (10) | 136 |

| | |
|---|---|
| Paige Felton (11) | 137 |
| Arvi Toth (11) | 138 |
| Aimee-Lei Jane Beckett (11) | 139 |
| Courtney Bradley (10) | 140 |
| Freya Ward (10) | 141 |
| Harry Weszka (10) | 142 |

# THE POEMS

# This Is Me

This is me, only me, this is what I have in me,
A drop of beauty,
A cup of funniness,
And finally a splash of love,
I've always tried to be myself,
Always tried my hardest, never doing bad and always helping,
What I love to do is be what I want,
Playing with other people.

- **M** e, I'm always me.
- **E** ncourage people all the time.

- **O** nly help the ones around me.
- **N** ow I play with the ones that don't have anyone.
- **L** onely people need someone kind.
- **Y** ou are special.

## Dalila Cortadellas Pascual (7)
Adamsrill Primary School, Sydenham

# Who Is Really Me?

Enter the Milky Way Galaxy,
Head down to Earth,
Zoom in on London in England,
To a young child at her birth.

Looking all over the room,
Eyes bright blue and round,
A tiny baby wondering where she is,
Observing what is around.
This is me.

Walking around a playground,
A child of one-ish,
Not interested in any of the toys,
Only the tank of fish.

"Fish," said the young child,
Speaking her very first word.
This started an eternal wordplay love,
Thank goodness it occurred.
This is me.

A cheerful toddler,
Aged only three,
In Cornwall on the golden sand,
Staring at the sea.

Now in her swimming costume,
Tumbling down the bay,
*Splash!* She landed in the sea,
And with water around her, life was okay.
This is me.

Freshly bought uniform,
Never worn before,
A four-year-old child wearing it,
Stepping through the front door.

Walking up the hill,
Hand in hand with her best friend,
It was her first day of school nursery,
And she never wanted the day to end.
This is me.

Now a few years older,
Skipping off to the park,

There to find her special tree,
When days felt too long or too dark.

Whenever she clambered,
She felt like she was free,
Its branches towering over her,
This amazing magical tree.
This is me.

Sitting down at the keyboard,
A confident eight-year-old girl,
Awaiting the sounds of beauty,
Musical notes as precious as pearls.

Never before had she played it,
Yet she knew it was a part of her,
And when she started playing,
Everything seemed a blur.
This is me.

A nine-year-old child at the top of a hill,
Staring at the bottom,
With a deep breath she hopped on her skateboard,
Hoping not to end up on her bottom.

The first time on a skateboard for her,
The first time a memory like this would be made,
But then *crash!* Off the board she fell,
At least now she knew the worst that could happen,
She was no longer afraid.
This is me.

An inquisitive child, the age of ten,
Sitting at the table,
Writing a piece of poetry,
Now that she is able.

I have explored my memories of the past,
But under my skin, who really is me?
I am a curious, wondrous, adventurous girl.

This is really me.

## Blythe Bell Lawrance (10)
Adamsrill Primary School, Sydenham

# Doggey Makes Me Happy!

**D** oggey makes me happy because I love him,
**O** n rainy days I hug him,
**G** one in the wash makes me sad,
**G** us, my dog likes him like I do,
**E** veryone who tries to swap a teddy for him, the answer is no!
**Y** oung, I am, but he is not.

**M** atted hair now but no he was fluffy before,
**A** dog bites him, I will not ignore,
**K** ayaking and he falls off, I swim down there,
**E** xciting but also washing once more,
**S** leeping, shh... I respect him.

**M** ayor of the city, I would vote for him,
**E** nergetic because he is a springer spaniel.

**H** e is love, he is warmth, I can't go anywhere without him,
**A** good dog, a kind dog, the dog you would love,
**P** eople don't respect him,
**P** eople say, "He's a bad dog," but no,
**Y** oung like me say Doggey nice.

## Isla Pym (8)
Adamsrill Primary School, Sydenham

# This Is Me!

This is a girl with a nature as bright as the sun,
A girl with eyes and hair as brown as bark,
And eyes filled with happiness, kindness and curiosity,
Like a jam doughnut.

I am a girl who loves whizzing around on her bike,
But crumples at the idea of a great big hike,
A girl who loves to write and read,
And doing helpful deeds.

I like to pretend to do magic,
But not spells that are tragic,
I am a girl who is a nature lover,
I am a girl who cares for the world,
And a girl who loves lots of animals,
I am a girl who is a detective at heart,
A girl who loves to curl up in a cosy corner,
And read until my eyes droop,
I love to write my own stories,
And keep my creativity stream flowing,

I am a colourful little girl,
Who wants to travel the world,
But finally:
This is me!

**Olive Yamaguchi-Crawley (10)**
Adamsrill Primary School, Sydenham

# This Is Me!

This is me,
As happy as can be,
Writing with glee,
For a poem about me!

This is me,
My name is Lola,
I am quite funny,
And I like Coca-Cola!

This is me,
I love playing with my friends,
Even though sometimes they drive me round the bend!

This is me,
I am from St Vincent Guyana and the land of Scots,
I like making noise for the NHS with pans and pots.

This is me,
I love to act, to dance and sing,

I am extremely unique,
(Style's my thing!)

This is me,
Skateboarding's my jam,
I love to make up handclaps,
Ones that go bang!

This is me,
Ending my poem,
Did you know that in Scotland right now it's snowing?

This is me,
I will see you next time,
I hope you liked my poem,
The poem that rhymed!

## Lola Haywood Williams (9)
Adamsrill Primary School, Sydenham

# My Imagination

A mind with care and a loving heart,
A mind with ideas big and small,
A mind with thoughts as large as the sun,
A mind with joy and laughter within.

A mind with tales sad and happy,
A mind with tales exciting and simple,
A mind with tales dark and grim,
A mind with tales glittering and golden.

A mind with memories bitter and cold,
A mind with memories of laughter and friendship,
A mind with memories of books good and bad,
In my mind this is me.

**Stella Jean Collings (9)**
Adamsrill Primary School, Sydenham

# This Is Me!

Look at me,
What do you see?
You see a face full of happiness and glee,
As I run around and flee.

Video games are now my life,
As in it, I release all of my strife,
I sit there and be snack man,
As I sit there and beat Pac-Man.

I'm always munching to victory,
As I sit here and learn history,
When I AFK for XP and loot,
I'm always eating a bowl of fruit.

This is me!

**Asher Bear (10)**
Adamsrill Primary School, Sydenham

# This Is Me

T his is me!
H ilariously,
I like to play games with my family,
S ometimes I laugh and be a silly monkey.

I 'm incredibly good on sports day,
S uper-duper funny when I mess around with my brother.

M y life is good and my parents are nice as ice cream,
E very day I take care of my cat and go on adventures.

**Daniel (7)**
Adamsrill Primary School, Sydenham

# A Recipe Of Kayla!

A pinch of talent,
Five tablespoons of sass (trust me)
A teaspoon of love,
A sprinkle of creativity.

Five millilitres of the pinch of talent,
Twenty millilitres of tablespoons of sass (per spoon)
Two teaspoons of love,
Fifty litres of creativity (per sprinkle)

Wa la!

**Kayla Oluwatobi (9)**
Adamsrill Primary School, Sydenham

# London

**L** eicester Square is my favourite place of mine!
**O** n my own I am extremely confident!
**N** ow I am brave from bullies,
**D** ancing is the worst of mine!
**O** n this planet I am stopping climate change,
**N** ewlands Park is the first place I know!

**Shahid Abbas (8)**
Adamsrill Primary School, Sydenham

# My Life

**T** all,
**H** appy as a boy on Christmas Day,
**I** ncredible,
**S** uper fun to play with.

**I** 'm very playful,
**S** illy.

**M** aking cakes,
**E** xcellent at running.

## Eli
Adamsrill Primary School, Sydenham

# Me

A girl,
Artistic,
Ten years old,
Black,
Caribbean,
Jamaican,
From Ireland,
Shy,
Quiet,
Strong,
Friendly,
This is me,
Who are you?

**Amanda Abiana Nelson (10)**
Adamsrill Primary School, Sydenham

# This Is Me

This is me,
I'm here can't you see?
I play football,
And played netball.
Though I don't like cats,
I kind of like rats.
I'm obsessed with the Scotland national team,
Football is kinda my theme.
Favourite player: John Mcginn,
You don't like him? That's a sin.
Dogs really are my thing,
Not to the point that I sing.

**Ben Davidson (11)**
Bankton Primary School, Dedridge

# My Saturday Morning

I woke up on a Saturday morning,
There was no time to play,
I had a game,
So I gotta get zooming,
It was already eight,
Luckily I wasn't running late,
I got into the car while I ate a Snickers bar,
I'm so lucky I don't live too far,
We played our game,
And gladly it didn't rain,
We got the win,
But I bruised my chin,
I got back home,
It felt like I broke a bone,
I got all clean,
And took a nap,
As my sister climbed on my lap,
She wakes me up,
And I got back up,
I practised on my piano to learn a new song,
But my sister interrupted with her loud bangs,

I wrote a poem as I'm doing right now,
It helps me turn my frown upside down,
I practise my drawings,
As I listened to my music,
My sister joined, it wasn't quite amusing,
I got really tired after a long day,
So I got some rest waiting for Sunday.

## Ethan Buendia (11)
Bankton Primary School, Dedridge

# All About Me
*A kennings poem*

Chocolate muncher,
Fast walker,
Secret keeper,
Truth teller,
TikTok creator,
TikTok watcher,
Loud talker,
McDonald's lover,
Football player,
Friend carer,
Fast writer,
Dog adorer,
Programme liker,
Sunset enjoyer.

**Ava Mcadam (11)**
Bankton Primary School, Dedridge

# Who Am I?

*A kennings poem*

Book reader,
Comic maker,
Cat lover,
Cat owner,
Minecraft gamer,
Among Us imposter,
Book writer,
Pizza eater,
Scratch coder,
Illustrat-er,
Lego builder,
Sushi gobbler,
(Non-alcoholic) coffee drinker,
Kennings writer.

**Kacey Koo (11)**
Bankton Primary School, Dedridge

# This Is Me

J elly filled,
A lways awesome to eat!
F antastic,
F attening,
A mazing.

C oncentrated cakes,
A lways makes me feel better,
K eep them safe,
E dible,
S crumptious.

**Kyle Robertson (11)**
Bankton Primary School, Dedridge

# This Is Me
*A kennings poem*

Friend maker,
Fortnite player,
YouTuber,
PlayStation 4 gamer,
Fondant lover,
Pet carer,
Chocolate muncher,
Scratch coder,
Lego builder,
Good painter,
Footballer,
Basketball shooter,
Friend lover.

## Robbie Vannet (11)
Bankton Primary School, Dedridge

# Who Am I?

I am a truth teller,
I am a friend maker,
I have a heart full of kindness,
I have a joyful life.

I am reliable,
I am valuable,
I have sympathy,
I have confidence.

I am vain,
I am trustworthy.

**Miral Yousif (11)**
Bankton Primary School, Dedridge

# This Is Me

*A kennings poem*

Secret keeper,
Music listener,
Quiet talker,
Chicken chewer,
Movie watcher,
BTS lover,
Hard worker,
Lemon muncher,
Fun maker,
Gift giver,
Great helper,
Basketball player.

**Rayan Krouma (11)**
Bankton Primary School, Dedridge

# Me In Life

I love video games,
Also riding in trains.
I enjoy Greek history,
And a good mystery.
I love to use Scratch,
And like a Hunger Games deathmatch.
I love swimming,
And have joy brimming.

**Caleb Craig (11)**
Bankton Primary School, Dedridge

# Who Am I?
*A kennings poem*

Blue lover,
Chocolate eater,
Friend maker,
Secret keeper,
Truth teller,
TikTok watcher,
Fast walker,
Dog lover,
Friend carer,
Fast writer,
Football player.

**Leah Jack (11)**
Bankton Primary School, Dedridge

# This Is Me
*A kennings poem*

Book reader,
Story writer,
Game player,
Glasses wearer,
Dog lover,
Joy bringer,
Phone user,
Kindness giver,
Pizza chomper,
Scratch coder,
Lego builder.

## Fraser Haw (11)
Bankton Primary School, Dedridge

# All About Me
*A kennings poem*

Football player,
PlayStation 5 gamer,
McDonald's eater,
Scratch coder,
Dog lover,
Cat hater,
Friend maker,
Car dreamer,
Outside explorer,
Ear lugger.

## Nathan Campbell (11)
Bankton Primary School, Dedridge

# About Lauren
*A kennings poem*

Anime watcher,
Cat owner,
Chocolate muncher,
Digital painter,
Football player,
Friend maker,
Happy singer,
Phone lover,
PlayStation 4 gamer,
TikTok user.

**Lauren Robertson (11)**
Bankton Primary School, Dedridge

# This Is Me

My favourite colour is red,
I love sleeping in my bed.
I am a chicken muncher,
I am a great hunter.
I love to eat,
Especially meat.
I like to be fair,
So I share.

## Taiba Ali (10)
Bankton Primary School, Dedridge

# Who Am I?
*A kennings poem*

Outside player,
Food muncher,
Future doctor,
Chocolate eater,
Secret keeper,
Friend maker,
Good listener,
Sun lover,
Confident talker,
TikTok watcher.

## Mirren Brown (11)
Bankton Primary School, Dedridge

# About Me
*A kennings poem*

Cat carer,
Great gamer,
Chocolate chomper,
Minecraft maker,
Easy eater,
Crazy coder,
Rapid reader,
Lego lover,
Hagfish hater,
Rubbish recycler.

**Daniel Friis Jørgensen (11)**
Bankton Primary School, Dedridge

# Kennings Poem

PlayStation 5 consoler,
Snack man,
Star Wars liker,
Marvel watcher,
Food lover,
FIFA gamer,
Football delighter,
Basketball fan,
Subnautica player.

**Cole Morrow (11)**
Bankton Primary School, Dedridge

# All About Me
*A kennings poem*

TikTok maker,
Programme liker,
Lemon muncher,
Horror lover,
Slow worker,
Quiet talker,
Secret keeper,
Tom Holland liker,
Vampire Diaries watcher.

**Isla Mowatt (11)**
Bankton Primary School, Dedridge

# I Am...

I am...
A good baker,
A creative fashion designer,

I am...
Playful,
Cheerful,

I like...
Using my electric scooter,
Who am I?

**Kayleigh Burrows**
Bankton Primary School, Dedridge

# Who Am I?

*A kennings poem*

Game player,
Lasagne eater,
Dog hugger,
School attender,
Aygo passenger,
Trend maker,
Book reader,
Bike rider,
Who am I?

**Daniel David Gough (12)**
Bankton Primary School, Dedridge

# This Is Me!
*A kennings poem*

Pizza eater,
Banana lover,
Kirby enjoyer,
Roblox player,
Idea maker,
Big imaginer,
Noise hater,
Video watcher.

**Nathan Snape (11)**
Bankton Primary School, Dedridge

# Thursday Nights

**G** oing every Thursday,
**Y** akking along with friends when waiting for our go,
**M** ats, beams, bars and vaults,
**N** ever giving up, even when it's hard,
**A** lways needing a drink,
**S** winging on the bars, forwards and backwards,
**T** rying as hard as we possibly can,
**I** love doing it, even though it can be tricky,
**C** an't wait for my next session,
**S** omersaulting on the bouncy, soft track.

## Erin Westwood (9)
Hasland Junior School, Hasland

# The Nature

Springtime songs fill the sky,
Dandelions dance during day,
Butterflies beautifully bump bees.

Rhododendrons house birds like a hotel,
Daisies dance in the breeze,
Martians miraculously move like mystical creatures.

Whirling winds are hurricanes,
Golden leaves are looming over beetles.

Winter wind whirl weeds,
Christmas trees outside light up the sky,
And the fresh cold breeze makes my lungs freeze.

**Kacey Pell (10)**
Hasland Junior School, Hasland

# Beautiful

You're sweet, you're kind, you're beautiful with everything you do!
Your smile, as bright as the sun itself,
With lips the rosy red colour.
You're beautiful, you really are!
The glowing hair upon your head,
Identical to a crown!
That's why I want to say you're just beautiful, just the way you are!

**Ava Wilkinson (9)**
Hasland Junior School, Hasland

# If I Had Fins

If I had fins I would swim through the ocean like a dolphin.
If I had fins I would glide through the ocean like a jellyfish.
If I had fins I would be a very quiet fish.
If I had fins I would be the kindest shark ever.
If I had fins I wouldn't be a bully.

### Ellie May Lilly Pell (10)
Hasland Junior School, Hasland

# All About Me

Born in a snowstorm,
A name that no one else has.
An anxious artist,
Reads as fast as cheetahs run.
Dancer in the winter sun.

## Darwyn Steele (8)
Hasland Junior School, Hasland

# My Little Brother

My little brother is small and cute,
He always makes me laugh.
We play together every day,
And ride our bikes out on the path.
He follows me around the house,
And crawls between my legs.
I can't ever say no to him,
He doesn't even need to beg.
I love my brother quite a lot,
He's growing really fast.
I hope we stay best friends forever,
And the fun times always last.

**Levent Kizilkaya (9)**
Kirkshaws Primary School, Coatbridge

# All About Me!

**K** ind and caring is who I am,
**A** lways going into things nice and calm,
**Y** oung and fun is how I come across,
**L** ikeable and sweet, just like candyfloss,
**E** ager to learn different skills in my team,
**I** nvested to keep at it, to live my dream,
**G** enerous and cheery is the way to be,
**H** appy and loved is why I am me.

**Kayleigh Angela Cunningham (9)**
Kirkshaws Primary School, Coatbridge

# I Am Me

Hands to help with,
Eyes to see,
I'm very happy with all of my might.
Ears to hear with,
Toes to touch and feel so free,
I'm very happy with all of me.
Nose to smell with,
Legs to climb,
I'm very happy with all of me.
I am growing as big as me.
I'm so very happy and this is me!

## Emily Paton (10)
Kirkshaws Primary School, Coatbridge

# Katie Paton Story

I am not for everybody,
I know my truth, I know who I am,
I know what I do and don't bring to school.
I'm not easy to handle,
But I do bring lots of happiness.
I bring love and care,
But I am not perfect,
And if I don't fit in with a group that is good with me.

## Katie Paton (10)
Kirkshaws Primary School, Coatbridge

# All About Me

**B** enevolent in every way,
**E** ager to learn,
**I** ntellectual human being,
**N** ice and generous to everyone,
**G** reatest hobby is gaming.

**M** indful to other people,
**E** nthusiastic and passionate about learning!

**Ethan Neville Madzinga (11)**
Kirkshaws Primary School, Coatbridge

# Who Is It?

My name starts with L,
I have brown shoulder-length hair,
My eyes are very dark and my skin is very pale,
I wear round glasses,
Can you guess, can you tell?
Lucas and Carlin are my BFFs,
Surely you must know who I am by this?

It is me!

**Lucy Bannister (10)**
Kirkshaws Primary School, Coatbridge

# Me

**K** ind,
**I** ndependent,
**A** glass full of love,
**R** ay of sunshine,
**A** nd a cup of curiosity.

## Kiara Puiu (9)
Kirkshaws Primary School, Coatbridge

# Nature Is Most Important!

My name is Zoe,
I can hear the seas and all the bees,
Slowly it fades away,
During the long day,
There are no sounds,
The sounds are out of bounds,
This is me, this is me,
The girl who cares about trees,
They chop them down,
That's when I can only frown,
We humans need to stop polluting,
We need to start recycling,
I'm blue as the sea,
When I can't see the trees,
We need to stop killing the planet.

**Zoe Williams (9)**
Middleton Primary School, Leeds

# A Volcanic Night

My mind is volcanic, my flames grow inside,
I'm the only one making noise on this silent night.
I need someone with me 'cause my room's like a library.
There is nothing at all,
My head's at the ceiling.
Does that mean I'm tall?
I'm like my hopes as high as can be.
We all walk the tightrope, don't you agree?
I always work hard so please let me go to sleep.

## Nathan Johnstone (10)
Middleton Primary School, Leeds

# This Is Me

This is me, this is me,
Not the biggest in the group,
But this is me, probably the saddest,
And also I'm a geek, not the oldest,
My name is Mason,
Yet with all that,
I've got a very lovely family,
And I'm grateful,
For my friends,
And playful pets,
This is a lovely beat,
This is me.

**Mason Fletcher (10)**
Middleton Primary School, Leeds

# Trapped

I feel locked into a small cramped box,
Stopped by an invisible force,
Edging closer to where the water falls,
I miss my friends and they miss me,
They are the ones that pulled me out the river,
I'm not smart but I'm quite clever,
But I got myself into this situation.

## Dean Speake (11)
Middleton Primary School, Leeds

# The Real Me

This is me, this is me, small little me,
I'm not tall, I'm actually small,
Small like a busy bee or maybe even a pea,
But I am Mia, not a bee or a pea,
I may be small, small as a ball,
But I am proud to be small,
Because this is me, the real Mia me.

## Mia Kalaszynska (9)
Middleton Primary School, Leeds

# Summer

I'm as yellow as the bright sun,
When I'm having fun,
All the flowers grow up high,
In the sky,
When it's summer,
It's way more funner,
I'm filled with joy and laughter,
In the afternoon before and after.

**Emmanuella Mouanjo (9)**
Middleton Primary School, Leeds

# All About Me

My hair is golden just like Goldilocks,
My eyes are blue just like the ocean,
I am brave and strong just like a lion,
I am kind and caring just like a nurse,
Each day I go to school to try my best,
And I will never do any less,
I will always do my homework and try my best,
Just like I do in every school test,
When I laugh I make people happy,
I am smart and can do many things,
One day I'll show the world how great I am,
When I spread my wings,
This is me!

**Eva Gilbert (9)**
Rolleston Primary School, Glen Parva

# Football

Sailing down the wing, Ronaldo's gonna sing,
Portugal, Portugal, he owns a big waterfall.

Oh back in goal, he's the best in the world,
No one can get past Mbappe, he can clap you any day.

Messi is the best, he doesn't need a rest,
Ronaldinho's learned a lesson, Neymar has the best car collection.

England won, Chelsea sucks, Barcelona is the best,
They always win, just by a little bit.

**Frayer Sluggett (10)**
Rolleston Primary School, Glen Parva

# This Is Me

**T** icklish as a monkey,
**H** as a heart of gold, I've been told,
**I** love roller skating on a Saturday with my nannie and grandad,
**S** upporting and loving my mum,

**I** can't wait for fish and chips Fridays at school,
**S** leeping with all my teddy bears on my bed makes me feel safe,

**M** aking memories,
**E** xcited to go to Brownies and getting my badges.

## Rosie Bond (9)
Rolleston Primary School, Glen Parva

# This Is Me

I am smiley and clever,
I am nice and sneaky,
I am helpful and happy,
I wonder if I'm going to be a rock hero in the future,
I wonder what my life is going to be like when I'm twenty-one,
I wonder if I get better at football,
I dream about getting a PlayStation 5,
I dream about being Lionel Messi,
I love my cats,
I love my school,
I love playing football.

## Isaac Wye (8)
Rolleston Primary School, Glen Parva

# This Is Me

My family is the best,
Number ten is even,
America is nice,
Makkah is beautiful and it's for all the Muslims,
Elephants are cute,
I love my family,
Sara is my best friend,
Penguins are adorable,
A dog can save your life,
Rolleston Primary School is the best,
I am a big sister,
Around my house is so beautiful.

## Paria Mohamdi (10)
Rolleston Primary School, Glen Parva

# I Love

I love dogs,
I love cats,
I love mice,
I love squirrels,
I love my mum,
I love my dad,
I love the beach,
I love going to Worcestershire,
I love going up Malvern hills,
I love my game,
I love school,
I love my house,
I love my PlayStation 4,
I love my room,
I love my family.

This is me!

**Daniel Derrett-Baugh (7)**
Rolleston Primary School, Glen Parva

# This Is Me!

I am just a girl with a big heart that loves to sing and dance,
My friends are cameras because whenever I look at them I smile,
I love myself and that's all that matters,
I hope someone will see this and I make them feel proud,
My favourite animals are all I have,
Two pets, a cat and a dog,
And I love them both very much.

## Emilia Hinz (9)
Rolleston Primary School, Glen Parva

# This Is My Life

I am a good gamer,
Also, I'm a good brother,
I love riding my scooter,
I like sweets,
I am a chocolate lover,
I like Fortnite,
I am a brilliant eater,
I am a fast eater,
I like ice cream,
I am a good bike rider,
Also like watching TV,
I like playing my PlayStation Four.

This is me!

**Leo Carolan (8)**
Rolleston Primary School, Glen Parva

# My Life

I am a...
Flexible person like elastic,
Animal lover,
Delightful drawer,
Fab daughter (and sister 'not')
Lovely singer,
Book worm,
Sporty person,
Great gamer,
I love nature,
My eyes are as blue as the ocean,
Last but not least,
My hair is as thick as a brick.

This is me!

## Alice Spence (8)
Rolleston Primary School, Glen Parva

# Me

I am me,
I am an older sister,
I am a friend,
I am me,
I am a daughter,
I am female,
I am strong,
I am me,
People say I am friendly,
People say I am caring,
People say I am helpful,
I am me,
I reach for the stars,
I aim for the best,
I am always on the positive side.

## Isabella Maeve Robson (10)
Rolleston Primary School, Glen Parva

# This Is Me!

T all person in my family,
H air is red like my jumper,
I am a dog lover like my dad,
S o I am a pizza liker like my sister.

I 'm a gamer like my uncle,
S o I like gaming.

M y mum and dad are the best,
E lso, my sister, is the best.

## Harley Mumford (8)
Rolleston Primary School, Glen Parva

# Me

I am a student,
I am me,
I am a middle child,
I am funny,
I am a friend,
I am a daughter,
I am me,
I am a girl,
I am fearless,
I am me,
People say I'm smart,
People say I am helpful,
I am never negative,
I am me,
I am Ellie-Mae Gracie!

**Ellie-Mae Pryor (9)**
Rolleston Primary School, Glen Parva

# This Is Me
*A kennings poem*

I am a chocolate eater,
I am an owl lover,
I am a crocodile hater,
I am a chicken,
I am a chatterboxer,
I am a pizza lover,
I am a burger lover,
I am a silly brother,
I keep my things in a safe place,
I am a gamer,
I am an art lover.

I am me!

## Charlie Lee Toon (9)
Rolleston Primary School, Glen Parva

# This Is Me

I am a lovely daughter,
I am a lovely sister,
I am a lovely friend,
I am a chocolate lover,
I am an egg hater,
I am the best BFF,
I am a good reader,
I am a gamer,
My hair is dark brown,
My eyes are dark brown.

This is me!

## Darci Rae Rayns (8)
Rolleston Primary School, Glen Parva

# About Me, Guess Who I Am?

I'm ginger, I'm pretty, I'm nice,
My name begins with an L and also I am a female,
My hobby is to cook cakes and cupcakes, yum! Yum!

You want to know? It is...
Lacey!

P.S. We have the best teacher ever, she is so nice like me.

## Lacey Mumford (10)
Rolleston Primary School, Glen Parva

# This Is Jake

J oyful as can be,
A mazing at horse riding,
K ind to others,
E xcellent at English.

H appy at school,
E xhilarating,
G ood at Roblox,
G reat at playing,
S ilent in school.

**Jake Thomas (9)**
Rolleston Primary School, Glen Parva

# All About Me
*A kennings poem*

I am an excellent reader.
I am a boy lover,
I am a chocolate lover.
I am a curly hair lover,
I am a pizza lover.
I am a rock legend,
I am a maths question lover.
I am a house lover,
I am a colouring lover.

This is me!

## Ayan Ben Grid (8)
Rolleston Primary School, Glen Parva

# What I Do

When I scream my bunny squeaks,
Every day I play,
When I play basketball I always get the ball,
When I was a kid I slid down slides,
When I am at school I need to snooze,
Every time I read I need to sleep,
When I see a cat I sit on a mat.

## Lexi Onions (8)
Rolleston Primary School, Glen Parva

# This Is Me

I'm an arty person,
I love to do arts and crafts,
I like to learn new things,
As I'm interested in new topics,
I love to dance around to my pop music,
I am also interested in the wildlife,
As I love my animals too.

**Abbey Corser Carlton (10)**
Rolleston Primary School, Glen Parva

# All About Me!

*A kennings poem*

I am a fab sister,
I am a loving daughter,
I am an animal adorer,
I am an art lover,
I am a fab family member,
I have a crazy colouring addiction,
I am a brilliant book reader,
I am a chocolate eater.
This is me!

**Brea-Mae Battle (8)**
Rolleston Primary School, Glen Parva

# This Is Me And My Dreams

I am smart and funny,
I wonder if I can be a sea captain,
Or be mayor,
I dream of being a team champion,
And meeting AJ Styles and Seth Rollins,
I wish I was a person who makes cars,
And want to be a teacher to help kids.

## Freddy
Rolleston Primary School, Glen Parva

# This Is Charlie

I am nice,
I am speedy,
I am strong,
I am funny,
I wonder what life will be like when I'm older,
I wonder who my new teacher will be,
I dream to be a superhero,
I love my family and friends.
This is me!

## Charlie Frearson (7)
Rolleston Primary School, Glen Parva

# Amazing Things About Me

*A kennings poem*

I am a,
Super footballer,
Harry Potter fan,
A book worm,
Super gamer,
Animal lover,
Pizza adorer,
Onion hater,
A good reader,
Excellent tennis player,
A good helper,
And a nice brother.

**Preston Underwood (9)**
Rolleston Primary School, Glen Parva

# This Is Me

I am an ice cream lover,
I am a nice sister,
I am a BFF,
I am a fab gamer,
I am a smart girl,
I am a book lover,
I am a pet owner,
I am a funny person,
My eyes are as brown as a tree,
This is me.

## Amelia Hancock (8)
Rolleston Primary School, Glen Parva

# Valour

I am strong, but solo,
I stare my fear in the eye,
I don't back off from a difficult fight,
I never ever give up even when I'm knocked down,
I am unstoppable,
What emotion am I?

Answer: Brave.

## Muaaz Imran (9)
Rolleston Primary School, Glen Parva

# This Is Me

*A kennings poem*

I am a football fan,
I am a fab footballer,
I am a big brother,
I am a chatterboxer,
I am a loving person,
I am a rock hero,
I am a fantastic super striker,
I am a super gamer.

This is me!

## Koby Keogh (9)
Rolleston Primary School, Glen Parva

# Amazing Things

I am a,
Superstar football player,
Fab brother,
Amazing magic tricker,
Book reader,
Amazing time table rockstar,
Creative lover,
Unbreakable bone,
And I'm a genius.

This is me!

**Bogdan Cernei (9)**
Rolleston Primary School, Glen Parva

# Born To Be A Warrior

**K** ind, Kyla was always a smiler,
**Y** ou wouldn't believe she was a survivor,
**L** ucky and brave and a pizza lover,
**A** great daughter and sister too.

This is me, a born survivor.

### Kyla Halifax (9)
Rolleston Primary School, Glen Parva

# This Is Me

**K** angaroo is my favourite animal in the world,
**O** reos are my favourite food,
**B** reaking a KitKat into two pieces,
**E** ven with everything I get,
**N** ever been hungry at home.

## Koben Smith (9)
Rolleston Primary School, Glen Parva

# I Am Me!

Ginger I am,
Unique I am,
Energetic I am,
Fearless I am,
Independent I am,
Courageous I am,
Hazel-eyed I am,
I'm not that person over there,
Or there,
I am,
Me!

**Taryn Perkins (10)**
Rolleston Primary School, Glen Parva

# All About Me

**M** indful every day,
**A** ctive always,
**R** eflective at everything,
**L** oveable forever,
**E** nergetic at playtimes,
**Y** oung in my heart.

This is me!

## Marley Wye (9)
Rolleston Primary School, Glen Parva

# About Me
*A kennings poem*

I am an owl lover,
I am a spider hater,
I am a brilliant reader,
I am a Harry Potter fan,
I am a rock legend,
I am a colouring lover,
I am a hamster lover.
This is me!

## Miley Moran (9)
Rolleston Primary School, Glen Parva

# All About Me!

I am confident, happy, successful,
I wonder what I will look like in the future, Heaven and the new days,
I dream about being a famous singer,
I love my family and my colourful bands.

**Sarah Fatah (8)**
Rolleston Primary School, Glen Parva

# A Day At School

E xcellent at math,
L oud noise I hate,
I ntelligent to be,
S cience is not my thing,
H istory's a bore,
A nd this is me!

**Elisha Baines (8)**
Rolleston Primary School, Glen Parva

# The Best Person Is

O utstanding scorer,
L ovely reader,
I mpeccable gamer,
V ague talker,
E pic at everything,
R unning monster.

**Oliver Redman (9)**
Rolleston Primary School, Glen Parva

# This Is Haira

**H** appy about my friends,
**A** ctive in gymnastics,
**I** nspirational at art,
**R** eally good at crafting,
**A** bsolutely everything.

**Haira Ihsan (8)**
Rolleston Primary School, Glen Parva

# This Is Me!

I am intelligent, I am crazy,
I am bubbly,
I wonder what life will be like in the future,
I dream about meeting a dolphin,
I love my personality.

### Esmé Branstone (8)
Rolleston Primary School, Glen Parva

# This Is Me

I am giggly,
I am fun,
I am happy,
I wonder what life will be like when I am older,
I dream about living with rainbows,
I love my mum.

## Molly Smith (8)
Rolleston Primary School, Glen Parva

# My Life

I am a good child,
I am my dad's star,
Also the best bike rider,
I have a sweet tooth,
Last but not least,
PlayStation 4 addict.

**Zayan Seedat (8)**
Rolleston Primary School, Glen Parva

# All About Me

I am fast,
I wonder what World War One was like,
I dream to meet Cristiano.
I love my cats.
This is me.

### Jesse Phillips (7)
Rolleston Primary School, Glen Parva

# This Is Me

Football is my favourite game,
I play it all the time, I practise night and day,
My favourite team is PSG,
I watch them when I can,
I clap and cheer when they win, I'm a big football fan,
I like to wear red, it's colour, that I love,
I like to visit Portugal, it's my favourite place to go,
Lisbon will be where I stay, big buildings and light shows,
My family are very important, I love them very much,
I like to make them happy and smile when I can,
This is a job I love.

This is me!

**Tonny Barreto (11)**
Thorpe Lea Primary School, Thorpe Lea

# Into The World

**P** urple is my favourite colour,
**O** ctopus is a favourite food,
**L** ovely,
**A** nd is kind.

**S** tarting to be a singer,
**T** ata is 'dad' in Polish,
**A** n amazing idea of sun in the moon,
**N** ice,
**K** ind,
**I** love my family,
**E** ggs are my favourite food,
**W** hich month was I born in?
**I** love my friend,
**C** zy lubie czarna czekolade albo biala
**Z** ebras are cool.

### Pola Stankiewicz (9)
Thorpe Lea Primary School, Thorpe Lea

# The Potion Of Me

**T** he potion on how to make me,
**H** andle fifty grams of happiness,
**I** nsert ten pounds of kindness,
**S** pray five sprays of love.

**I** n goes a bowl of diabetes,
**S** eparate my love of animals from my love of comics.

**M** ix them together,
**E** xcellent, you're done.

**E** xtra ingredients,
**L** ove of dogs, ten grams,
**L** ove of school,
**A** ll ingredients, easy to find.

**Ella Wells (10)**
Thorpe Lea Primary School, Thorpe Lea

# This Is Me!

**M** y favourite animal is a monkey,
**A** pples are nice when they are cut,
**D** onkeys are stinky,
**I** sabelle is my best friend forever and ever,
**S** ometimes I can be cheeky like a monkey,
**O** ranges are my least favourite fruit,
**N** ever be a bully.

**J** am is the worst, I don't like it,
**O** rlaith is my godsister,
**N** ever be unkind,
**E** at fruit,
**S** ometimes I'm naughty.

**Madison Jones (8)**
Thorpe Lea Primary School, Thorpe Lea

# All About Me

This is a poem all about me,
One that I'd really love you to see,
I love swimming and winning,
And I really love maths,
Which will definitely help me in my SATs,
I like it calm and quiet,
Not much of a riot,
Sometimes loud and crazy,
It's just amazing,
Now that you know all about me,
Feel free to come and see,
The wonderful person I am,
The wonderful person I'll be.

**Rashida Moortasa (11)**
Thorpe Lea Primary School, Thorpe Lea

# This Is My Life!

T ime to sing and dance and play,
E ven if I'm not okay,
A nd my friends and family,
G oing to keep me very happy,
A nd play day after day,
N ever missing a nice hot sunny day.

W e love our friends and family,
E ven if they are very angry,
S ometimes they are nice and kind,
T ime to open up my eyes.

**Teagan West (9)**
Thorpe Lea Primary School, Thorpe Lea

# This Is My Universe

**R** ed is my least favourite colour,
**A** mong Us is my second favourite game,
**Y** ellow is my baby sister's colour,
**Y** ousuf Primary School was my old school,
**A** aron is my friend,
**N** ight-time is when I go to sleep.

**S** hah is my surname,
**H** eights are fun,
**A** t home I do maths,
**H** eat makes me sweat.

**Rayyan Shah (9)**
Thorpe Lea Primary School, Thorpe Lea

# My Sleep Obsession

**L** ayla loves sleeping,
**A** ll comfortable in bed,
**Y** ou see Layla always wants to sleep,
**L** ovely soft sheets,
**A** mazing, fluffy pillows.

**L** ots of zzzs and cold chills,
**O** h no, alarm clock's ringing,
**V** ery sleepy indeed,
**E** very day is worth sleeping,
**S** leeping is like dreaming.

**Layla Rose Stevens (11)**
Thorpe Lea Primary School, Thorpe Lea

# This Is Me

I like football,
And all my friends are cool,
Pandas are cool,
Some people think they're fools,
I go to school every day,
Just to play with my friends all day,
My mum drives me in a car,
And says it is quite far,
Manchester United will win,
With a big grin,
I'm good at TT Rockstars,
And some people can be pop stars.

## Allyna (9)
Thorpe Lea Primary School, Thorpe Lea

# This Is Me!

*A kennings poem*

I am a...
Drawer,
iPad and Nintendo Switch player,
Cake maker,
Swimmer,
Rollerblader,
Cat owner,
Was a dog owner,
Noise maker,
Food eater,
TikTok watcher,
Koala lover,
Spider hater,
Horse rider,
Hoola hooper,
Hard worker,
Painter,
And finally...
A harmonica player!

**Maisie (9)**
Thorpe Lea Primary School, Thorpe Lea

# This Is Me!

**L** illy is my name,
**I** have cupcakes,
**L** ove spending time with my family,
**L** ike crafting,
**Y** ear four is the best class.

**J** ane is my middle name,
**A** nd I love ice cream!
**N** ever take it away from me!
**E** very day I wake up and have a party!

## Lilly Rickwood (9)
Thorpe Lea Primary School, Thorpe Lea

# This Is Me

**H** uns and guns,
**I** tems and Romans,
**S** uch a waste against barbarians,
**T** ime passes, empires rise, some fall to unwise demise,
**O** thers lie on the sidelines, waiting for a rainy day,
**R** omanize the east till the fifteenth century,
**Y** et these don't exist today.

## Antonio Rebenciuc (10)
Thorpe Lea Primary School, Thorpe Lea

# This Is Me

I like to play games,
And I like to make programmes day to day,
Listening to bagpipes, typing code,
My favourite animal is a toad.

I like maths problems that I can solve,
But a little too easy, it makes me bored.

I hope you enjoyed my poem,
Now it's time for me to go.

**Abdul Rahman Ali (10)**
Thorpe Lea Primary School, Thorpe Lea

# This Is Me!
*A kennings poem*

I am a...
Football player,
Tottenham lover,
PlayStation 4 player,
Keyboard player,
FIFA 2022 player,
Skateboard lover,
Dog lover,
A nice guy,
Piano player,
Football lover,
Pizza eater,
Cat lover,
Ice cream eater,
Chips eater.

**Roman Bartram (9)**
Thorpe Lea Primary School, Thorpe Lea

# Chelsea

**C** helsea's coming your way,
**H** olland you're gonna pay,
**E** veryone get out the way,
**L** ondon knows our name,
**S** ee us Blues at Stamford Bridge,
**E** ven if you support Cambridge,
**A** rsenal you're getting baited!

## Freddy Breach (11)
Thorpe Lea Primary School, Thorpe Lea

# Let's Go Shopping!

Happiness... £L
Intelligence... £O
Uniqueness... £L
Long hair... £A

Fashion sense... £L
Hard work... £E
Enthusiasm... £E

Total cost:
Lola Lee
Thanks for shopping!

**Lola Williamson (10)**
Thorpe Lea Primary School, Thorpe Lea

# This Is Me!

**F** astest person in the class,
**I** 'm kind to one another,
**N** o one is faster than me in my class,
**L** ewis is my brother's name,
**E** li is my best friend,
**Y** oghurt is my favourite.

**Finley William (8)**
Thorpe Lea Primary School, Thorpe Lea

# Things That I Love!
*A kennings poem*

I am a...
Football player,
Tottenham supporter,
Burger eater,
BMX bike rider,
Dog lover,
Skateboarder,
TikTok maker,
And finally...
Cookie and cream ice cream eater!

## Poppy R (9)
Thorpe Lea Primary School, Thorpe Lea

# This Is Me!
*A kennings poem*

I am a...
Switch player,
Football player,
Tottenham supporter,
Book reader,
Swimmer,
Skateboard rider,
Burger eater,
And finally...
A good Fortnite player!

## Taylan Basaran (8)
Thorpe Lea Primary School, Thorpe Lea

# This Is Me!

**F** ilip is my name,
**I** love to play games,
**L** ove Fridays,
**I** like pizza,
**P** ola is my friend.

## Filip Bartosiak (8)
Thorpe Lea Primary School, Thorpe Lea

# This Is Me!
*A kennings poem*

I am a...
Night-time waker
Pizza eater
Pasta lover
Good little helper
And finally...
A good friend.

**Alexis-May Hiley (8)**
Thorpe Lea Primary School, Thorpe Lea

# Perfect Family (Rap)

Three kids, mum and dad,
Big house, dog and cat,
Cool school but,
I don't live like that you see...
"You're rude, you're annoying!"
"You linger around like no one's seen ya!"
Kept on calling out to my father, but,
I must've been dumbstruck,
'Cause he didn't hear me for two years,
I went to foster care without warning,
And before I knew it, I was there in the morning,
I went to tea
The moment I set foot in the house, I felt free,
I have gone through a lot but,
I never kept my mouth shut,
I kept calling out,
And sometimes I had to shout,
You'll never see me hiding again,
For my friends picked me up when I was lost,
But now,
I am found.

**Lily Jayde Leeming (11)**
Unity Academy, Blackpool

# This Is Happy Me

**T** his is me, I'm more happy than a cat, meow,
**H** aving a sleep, I love going to bed,
**I** 'm caring like a wolf's mother to her kids,
**S** haring, I love to eat cheese.

**I** 'm funny like a comedian,
**S** howing my crazy mouse side.

**H** appiness and craziness, I like,
**A** ppearing out of nowhere,
**P** eople love me,
**P** eering over the hedge like a spy,
**Y** ou're gonna miss me.

**M** y parents love me,
**E** verybody cares for me.

### Dylan Pace (11)
Unity Academy, Blackpool

# My Favourite Dessert

It's hot but cold as ice,
And time is its enemy,
Don't eat too much or you'll get a brain freeze,
Sweet but sickly,
The colours of the famous zebra,
I suggest eating it with a spoon,
Melting like a snowman in summer,
If it melts, what a bummer,
Get both flavours, such a delight,
The taste of vanilla and chocolate,
And the best place to eat it is... bed!
The answer is chocolate fudge ice cream,
Everyone likes chocolate ice cream,
I would scream to get some,
Now tell me yours.

## Bella Precious (10)
Unity Academy, Blackpool

# Different

Even though I'm different,
Not like anyone else,
Not like average people,
Not even like a mouse,
I speak out loud to others,
I say when things aren't right,
Sometimes I get excited,
All the way in and out,
Even though I'm different,
No one ever shouts,
They find it all normal,
They do without a doubt,
With my two best friends,
Adventures never end,
Some are good,
Some are bad,
Even though I'm different,
I'm happy, I'm me.

**Lucia Panayiotis (11)**
Unity Academy, Blackpool

# Five More Minutes?

As I lie, sleeping in my bed,
Dreaming, about the mustard man,
"School time!" my father says,
And as I chow down, on a wooden flask,
I wake up, slowly, and wearily ask,
"Five more minutes, please?"
Though I know this feat would not,
Come as an ease,
"No! Get out of bed!"
And as I exit, my kingdom, my palace,
My limbs feel like solid lead,
And as I get dressed, my only solace,
Is that when I get home, I can go back to bed.

## Harlee Saunders (11)
Unity Academy, Blackpool

# This Is Me!

A game of football and a bit of sweat,
A pinch of McDonald's,
Five grams of laughter,
Ten pounds of games,
A page of Harry Potter,
A speck of models.

Now you need to:
Add a game of football and a bit of sweat,
Mix a page of Harry Potter,
Stir in roughly a pinch of McDonald's,
Finally, mix in a speck of models and give me a shake,
Put me in the oven at one hundred and eighty degrees and let me bake,
Once I have risen, I am complete!

**Tyler Cook (10)**
Unity Academy, Blackpool

# The Recipe For Me!

To make me you'll need:
The largest ice cream cone ever,
Ten pounds of autism,
A dazzle of comedy,
One thousand sprinkles,
A drop of mischief,
A really loud bell,
Ten grams of smart.

Now:
Get the ice cream and add ten pounds of autism,
Cover the ice cream in sprinkles and slide in a dazzle of comedy,
Place a really loud bell next to the ice cream and add a drop of mischief,
Finally, add fifty grams of smart.

This is me!

## Dylan Russell (11)
Unity Academy, Blackpool

# This Is Me

**T** rue friendship is the best thing in the world,
**H** aving my favourite food is my passion,
**I** ce cream is my favourite dessert of all time,
**S** leeping is the best time to lie down and relax.

**I** would love to work at KFC when I am older,
**S** ummer is the season to be sizzling.

**M** y favourite style of fashion is to be girly,
**E** mily is my best friend, we'll be pals forever!

## Freya Chennells (11)
Unity Academy, Blackpool

# How To Create Me

To create me you will need:

A dash of excitement,
A sprinkle of mischief,
A pinch of fun,
Ten pounds of happiness.

Now you need to:
Add a messy room,
Mix in a revision army,
Whilst stirring slowly pour a vibrant personality,
With a dash of emotions - mostly happiness, maybe sadness,
Carefully place onto a baking tray,
Bake at one-hundred and eighty degrees for thirty minutes.

**Paddy Jones (11)**
Unity Academy, Blackpool

# I Am Unique

I am different, I am unique,
No one is the same as me,
I could climb to the highest peak,
I'm unstoppable, you'll see.

Also, I love to draw,
My favourite colour is dark blue,
And there's more,
I love to watch Doctor Who.

I am different, so are you,
You are who you are,
Let all your dreams come true,
We are bright like shining stars.

**Elizer Oneall (11)**
Unity Academy, Blackpool

# This Is Me!

I am me, I am no other,
I am not like my sister or my brother,
I am new, I am not old,
As my story has never been told,
My life is mine, yours is yours,
As is the dinosaurs,
I fill my mind with things I like,
Football, FIFA, although I don't have a very good strike,
This is my life, yours is yours,
It ends like the dinosaurs,
Make it fun!

### Dylan Fallows (11)
Unity Academy, Blackpool

# This Is My Cat!

This is my cat,
She is a sphinx,
She hates new people,
She hates new food,
If you see her please be careful!
She will make your life a living hell!
She may look sweet, but,
She is a devil,
She will look at you and you will turn to stone,
She is my bodyguard,
She will protect,
If you do something to me,
She will become your threat!

**Keeley Royle (11)**
Unity Academy, Blackpool

# Me And My Team!

I am the tiger of my team,
I roar at them with all my steam,
History is for us to make!
We score goals and don't hesitate,
We help each other with pride and joy,
Whether a girl or boy!
I have fun playing with them,
We are best friends until then,
Until the end we wish each other good luck,
After the games we are covered in muck!

**Tillie Gilbert (10)**
Unity Academy, Blackpool

# I Love My Family

**T** he birthdays of mine are the best,
**H** olidays are fun,
**I** like cars so much,
**S** ometimes my uncle comes to my house.

**I** love my mom and dad lots,
**S** ometimes I go to the beach.

**M** y family are amazing,
**E** specially on day trips.

**Domonic Woodall (10)**
Unity Academy, Blackpool

# Artsy

I may be good at art,
Kind of like most people,
Very good at art!
Not like most people.
I may be quite different,
Perfect in every way.
My ideal people,
Most don't stay.
Everyone is different,
All in their own way.
This may affect some others,
Others in each way.

**Marika Pokule (10)**
Unity Academy, Blackpool

# This Is Me!

**T** he best midfielder in football!
**H** ungry every two seconds,
**I** 'm such a good friend,
**S** uch a good helper.

**I** am really shy!
**S** o good at everything I do.

**M** aybe a bit crazy,
**E** verything I do makes me proud of myself!

**Madeleine Green (10)**
Unity Academy, Blackpool

# My Dream!

**N** o, I'm not the person to waste time,
**U** sing my skills will save lives,
**R** esting is important but once I'm awake I'm focused on my goal,
**S** o, I must be wise whilst I focus on my dreams and goals,
**E** ven when tough things get in the way, I will be focused.

## Emily Moore (10)
Unity Academy, Blackpool

# Things About Me!

**F** ood is extremely good!
**A** lot of things I do: I help out, I am a good girl,
**M** arvellous but mischievous little one,
**I** love my family and friends,
**L** ove spending time with my pets,
**Y** ou are always going to get listened to when you are around me.

**Paige Felton (11)**
Unity Academy, Blackpool

# All About Me

A rchitecture is my favourite thing at home to do,
R ibena is unhealthy and it is unhealthy for animals,
V ertical shapes in maths are my favourite thing to do,
I am a good singer and it's really fun to do - it also helps my vocals.

## Arvi Toth (11)
Unity Academy, Blackpool

# Everything About Me!

I am a fun master,
I am an art lover,
I am a ponytail wearer,
I am going to be a pilot when I'm older,
I am a game player,
I am a foodie lover,
I am a speedy car admirer,
I am an animal lover,
My... my life is a wonder.

**Aimee-Lei Jane Beckett (11)**
Unity Academy, Blackpool

# This Is Me!

C aring and kind,
O rganised and chatty or so they say,
U nbeatable and friendly,
R eady to do anything,
T rying different things,
N ice,
E ager,
Y oung and free.

**Courtney Bradley (10)**
Unity Academy, Blackpool

# Things About Me!

**F** unny, nice, awesome,
**A** ll attention is on us,
**M** um is the best,
**I** love my family,
**L** oves to help out all the time,
**Y** ou will always get listened to.

**Freya Ward (10)**
Unity Academy, Blackpool

# This Is Me

*A kennings poem*

I am a food lover,
I am a sports player,
I am a game lover,
And I am a hard worker.

I am a rugby player,
I am a team player,
I am a front liner,
And this is me.

**Harry Weszka (10)**
Unity Academy, Blackpool